ABOUT PHOBIAS

Library of Congress Cataloging in Publication Data

Stein, Sara Bonnett.
    About Phobias.

    (The Open family series)
    SUMMARY: Uses separate text for adult
and child to explain that children's phobias are related
to their sexual feeings towards their parents.
    1. Fear in children—Juvenile literature.
2. Oedipus complex—Juvenile literature.
3. Electra complex—Juvenile literature.
[1. Oedipus complex.   2. Electra complex.
3. Phobias]
II. Stone, Erika.   III. Media Projects
Incorporated.   IV. Title.
BF723.F4S73   1979   158   78-65615
ISBN 0-8027-6348-0

First published in the United States of America in
1979 by the Walker Publishing Company, Inc.

Published simultaneously in Canada by Beaver-
books, Limited, Pickering, Ontario

ISBN 0-8027-6348-0

Library of Congress Catalog Card Number; 78-65615

Printed in the United States of America

ABOUT PHOBIAS

An Open Family Book For Parents And Children Together

by Sara Bonnett Stein

Thomas R. Holman,
Ph.D., Consultant
Psychologist, Postgraduate Center
for Mental Health, New York, New York

Photographs by Erika Stone

Walker and Company
New York, New York
Created by Media Projects Incorporated

A Note About This Book

When your child was a baby, you took him to the doctor to have him immunized for childhood illnesses. The injections hurt a little, but you knew they would prepare his body to cope with far more serious threats in the future. Yet there are other threats as painful and destructive to a child's growth as physical illness: Separation from his parents, a death in the family, a new baby, fears and fantasies of his own imagining that hurt as much as pain itself. These Open Family Books are to help adults prepare children for common hurts of childhood.

Caring adults try to protect their child from difficult events. But still that child has ears that overhear, eyes that read the faces of adults around him. If people are sad, he knows it. If people are worried, he knows it. If people are angry, he knows that too.

What he doesn't know—if no one tells him—is the whole story. In his attempts to make sense of what is going on around him, he fills in the fragments he has noticed with fantasied explanations of his own which, because he is a child, are often more frightening than the truth.

We protect children because we know them to be different, more easily damaged than ourselves. But the difference we sense is not widely understood. Children are more easily damaged because they cannot make distinctions yet between what is real and what is unreal, what is magic and what is logic. The tiger under a child's bed at night is as real to him as the tiger in the zoo. When he wishes a bad thing, he believes his wish can make the bad thing happen. His fearful imagining about what is going on grips him because he has no way to test the truth of it.

It is the job of parents to support and explain reality, to guide a child toward the truth even if it is painful. The dose may be small, just as a dose of vaccine is adjusted to the smallness of a baby; but even if it is a little at a time, it is only straightforwardness that gives children the internal strength to deal with things not as they imagine them to be, but as they are.

To do that, parents need to understand what sorts of fears, fantasies, misunderstandings are common to early childhood—what they might expect at three years old, or at five, or seven. They need simpler ways to explain the way complicated things are. The adult text of each of these books, in the left-hand column, explains extraordinary ways that ordinary children between three and eight years old attempt to make sense of difficult events in their lives. It puts into words uncomplicated ways to say things. It is probably best to read the adult text several times before you read the book to your child, so you will get a comfortable feel for the ideas and so you won't be distracted as you talk together. If your child can read, he may one day be curious to read the adult text. That's all right. What's written there is the same as what you are talking about together. The pictures and the words in large print are to start the talking between you and your child. The stories are intense enough to arouse curiosity and feeling. But they are reasonable, forthright and gentle, so a child can deal with the material at whatever level he is ready for.

The themes in these Open Family Books are common to children's play. That is no accident. Play, joyous but also serious, is the way a child enacts himself a little bit at a time, to get used to events, thoughts and feelings he is confused about. Helping a child keep clear on the difference between what is real and what is fantasy will not restrict a child's creativity in play. It will let him use fantasy more freely because it is less frightening.

In some ways, these books won't work. No matter how a parent explains things, a child will misunderstand some part of the explanation, sometimes right away, sometimes in retrospect, weeks or even months later. Parents really can't help this fact of psychological life. Nothing in human growing works all at once, completely or forever. But parents can keep the channels of communication open so that gradually their growing child can bring his version of the way things are closer to the reality. Each time you read an Open Family Book and talk about it together, your child will take in what at that moment is most useful to him. Another day, another month, years later, other aspects of the book will be useful to him in quite different ways. The book will not have changed; what he needs, what he notices, how he uses it will change.

But that is what these books are for: to open between adult and child the potential for growth that exists in human beings of all ages.

Every morning Susie climbs into bed with her mother and father.

We all know children who are scared of dogs, or bugs or germs. Such fears, whether they are mild and transient or crippling and permanent, are called phobias. They are so common that they can be considered an expected disturbance in the course of many children's development.

Usually an easy explanation is available: The child was actually bitten by a dog or stung by a bee. Although such events may well trigger a phobia, they are improbable causes. If a child is hit by a bicycle, he might become more cautious, but he is unlikely to refuse to leave the house for fear a bike might get him.

Because childhood is so filled with fears of the dark, and of thunder and kidnappers, we might be tempted to include phobias in the list of non-alarming anxieties. But the sudden onset of a phobia, the intensity of the fear, and the constraints it imposes on the child's everyday life are different. A phobia is alarming.

This story is an attempt to explain a phobia in a child of four in a way that reveals both underlying causes and an eventual resolution. The story— the story behind all boys' and girls' earliest phobias—is about the sexual feelings children normally express toward their parents. Sexuality in young children may be quite dif-

ficult to accept. It is hoped that the clarity and healthiness of Susie's feelings will lead to acceptance, and to the understanding needed to help a phobic child recover from his fears.

But Mommy says, "You are getting too old for this kind of cuddling. And too old to suck that thumb too."

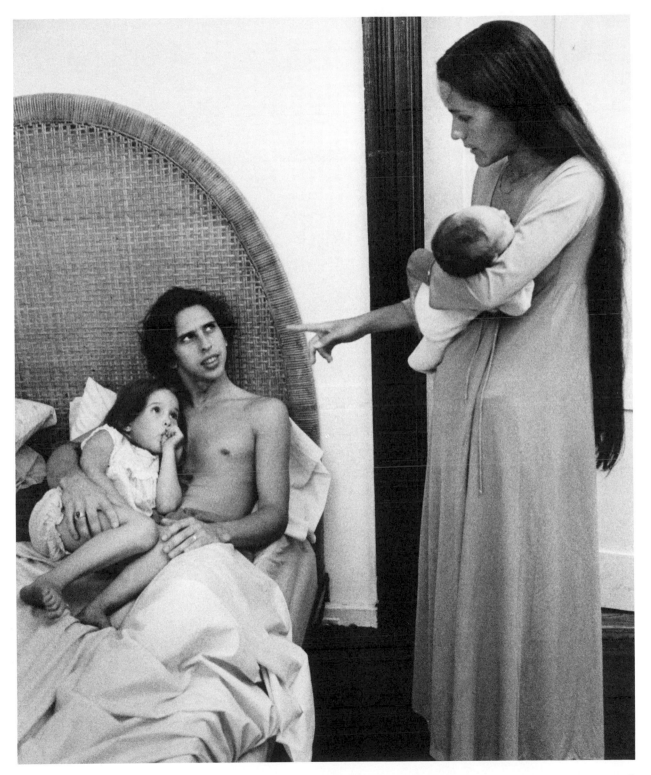

Toddlers rarely develop phobias, nor usually do children of elementary school age. Animal phobias are typical of the childhood years from two and a half to about five. The other phobias—of heights or of closed or open spaces—belong to adolescence and adulthood.

Here, in the bare flesh, warm smells, and enthusiastic caresses of young sensuality, is the context in which common phobias arise. Some of us may remember the sensations of such times of intimacy with a parent from our own childhood. More usually those days are forgotten, and we can only believe in them at all because we participate—as parents now—in similar scenes with our own loved children.

The sensual love a child feels toward a parent of the opposite sex—and its reciprocation—and the mild irritation it provokes in the other parent are normal and needed. Nevertheless, were a child's love less passionate there would not be fuel for fear. There would, of course, not be fuel for later love relationships either. The course of Susie's development, as of all children's, requires that she love her father (or a boy his mother) with passion, with a wish to be alone with him, with the hope of marrying him. A strong first love, though given up in time, is the source of strong love in adulthood.

So we can't deny a child the context in which a phobia arises; we can only deal with it sensitively when and if it happens.

Susie loves to watch Daddy in the bathroom. Mommy doesn't like that either.

Susie goes with Daddy to the bus stop when he leaves for work. He gives her a piggyback ride.

He lets her down to play with Butch. Butch jumps on Susie and licks her face. Susie can't wait until she has a puppy of her own.

It is important to understand that phobias are not "catching" from parent to child. Susie's parents are not overprotective, anxious, or phobic themselves. Nor is Susie a timid child.

In fact, this little girl is crazy about dogs. She screws up her face with pleasure as Butch licks her. She lets him jump on her. And her dearest wish is to have a puppy of her own. Exactly this excited admiration of dogs who bounce and lick and wag their tails will determine her choice of phobia later in the story. If her fascination were rather for little bugs and salamanders, she would likely choose them to fear; or horses, if they were her passion; or dirt and "germs," were that her secret delight. It is impossible to develop a phobia around an object that did not previously afford pleasure.

"I am staying with Grandma tonight," Mommy says. "Maybe you and Daddy can look at puppies tomorrow."

Susie has often wished to be alone with her daddy, to play at being his wife. Yet something worries her. The closer the wish seems to coming true, the more Susie has to worry about its consequences. Maybe a little girl can't handle the kind of hugging and kissing she senses are part of grown-up love. Surely a mommy who is annoyed at cuddling would not approve of marriage. And if Susie were to replace her mother, who would be around to take care of her? Such concerns don't erase a little girl's urges, but they pair them with anxiety.

All boys and girls, from the time they first court the parent of the opposite sex at about age three to the time they "swear off" sex and marriage at about age six, play out this conflict of passion and fear in games, dreams, actions, and symptoms.

Phobia is one possible symptom. Like all symptoms, it is designed not to cause pain but to relieve anxiety. This, for instance, is the way a dog phobia works: Dogs tend to remind children of their own excited romping, their own urges to lick and bite. That's why children take such pleasure in them. If a child becomes terrified of dogs—avoids seeing them or participating in their play—he protects himself from those excited feelings. What is more, his anxiety is relieved because he simultaneously punishes himself for his urges by the fear he feels. And he retreats to safety in another way as well: If he must cling to his parents to protect him, he is more like a baby again than a child pursuing his love.

Susie doesn't like it when Mommy isn't home. She gets worried. She can't sleep.

The episode of Susie being allowed to share her father's bed while his wife is away is here as a warning that behavior a child can see as seductive can go too far. To Susie, this seems more than a chummy morning cuddle—and we must try to see it in the raw as she does: Her father, half-nude and in a caressing mood, invites his daughter into bed.

In the rigid moral balance by which young children measure such stolen pleasures, retribution will weigh equally heavy. It is possible, though not predictable, that without this extra fillip of intimacy the phobia to follow could not have come to be. As it is, Susie needs only a source for an unconscious "idea:" the event that will precipitate her phobia.

Daddy lets her sleep in bed with him.

"In the morning," says Daddy, "we'll go to see the puppies."

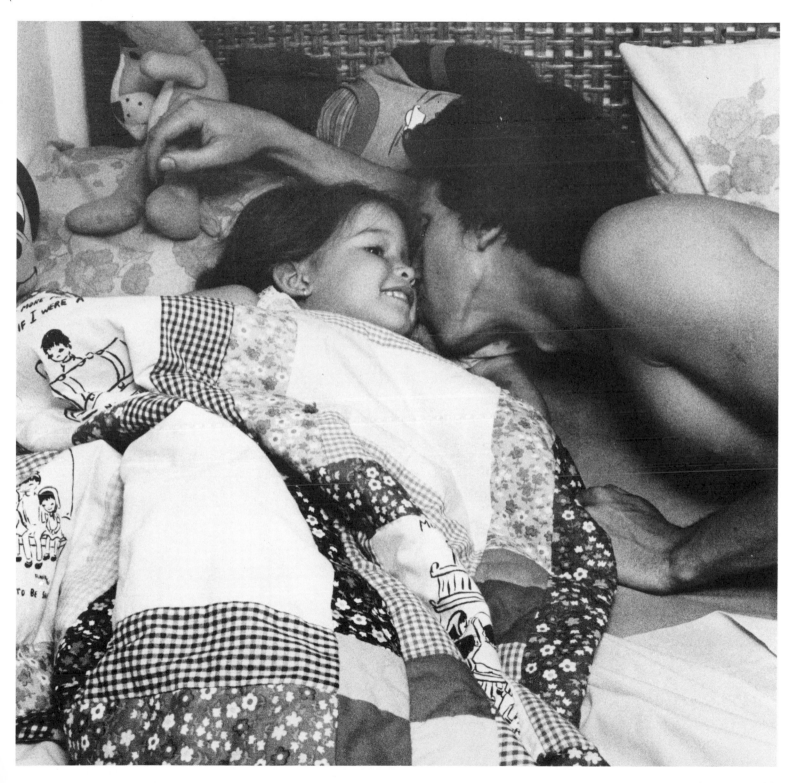

Here is the precipitating event: The mother dog growls and snaps at Susie.

If we look at the episode in the simplest way, it is at least scary. If we look at it more analytically, we can see it as even more serious. Susie was touching one of the puppies, lifting it from the cage, intending eventually to take it away from its mother. Susie's own mother has recently had a baby too. The resemblance between Susie's wish to take the puppy and her wish to take her mother's place as Daddy's wife—perhaps complete with a baby of her own—is inescapable. When girls have such wishes, Susie must have thought, mothers can be dangerous.

The puppies love Susie. But the mother dog growls and snaps her teeth. Daddy says she doesn't want anyone to take her puppies.

To Susie's father, her sudden fear of her old friend, Butch, may not be alarming. Like any of us, he doesn't acknowledge the change in her behavior right away and tries to dismiss it with common logic. Butch only wants to play; barking is a dog's way of talking, his mouth is open because he's panting. Although we as adults have to contribute the reality of our own perceptions, it simply does not get through to a child suffering such anxiety. Other attempts to influence a child's reactions by shaming him with names like "silly" and "sissy," or forcing him to approach or touch the dog, will damage our alliance with our child. When we can see that a child is frightened, the best move is to sympathize, protect, and wait to see what happens next.

When they get home again, Butch is waiting.

Suddenly, Susie is scared.

Her father thinks she's being silly.

Butch only wants to play.

Phobic symptoms can be mild, no more than an aversion to the object. Or they can be moderate, a visible nervousness when dogs are around. Or the terror a child feels can be so severe that he must pile up protective restrictions to the extent that his everyday life is crippled.

Mild aversion can also escalate to an inability to leave the house alone; and any of the symptoms may be as brief as a few weeks or as long as a whole childhood. Traces of unresolved phobias may last into adulthood.

Most prolonged and severe phobias occur in families in which parents suffer related anxieties. When a phobia seems intractible, professional help may be needed to make everyone feel better.

Once alert to the problem, Susie's family will manage well enough.

Mommy has come home. Everyone is busy. "Go outside and play," they tell Susie.

These are the steps Susie's parents will have to take to help their daughter out. First, they will have to admit that she has a problem. As we all know, that is hard enough. Second, they will have to realize that a phobia is a poor solution to a problem. To them, Susie's inability to go outside alone will be a nuisance. And to Susie, neat as her symptom is in that it simultaneously expresses both her wish and its retribution, her phobia is only a psychological stopgap. Unless the issues that cause symptoms are resolved, the symptoms themselves spread or escalate. Needless to say, resolution is the healthier way.

The third step is to get at the causes: by "listening" both to Susie's actions and to her words, by reviewing what general information on child development is available to them, and by putting the two together.

As to the resolution itself, we cannot do that for the child. But once we have a grasp of the problem, we can support a child's efforts toward resolution by intelligent conversation with the child, and by changes in our own behavior toward him.

But Susie can't go outside.
She sees Butch out there.

To hear what children mean, we must both watch and listen. And participate. Susie's mother listens—without contradicting—to a change of heart about puppies. In the next few pages she will notice a telling episode with the balloon, and later hear its echo in a scary dream. She will participate in these images through a mommy/puppy game.

Will she, like a professional, be able at last to make a coherent statement as to the cause of Susie's phobia? Not at all. More like a poem, these impressions will leave her with sensibilities she did not have before. This is enough. Susie will be able to make use of a relatively small amount of communication through words, play, and attitude to re-establish the healthy course of her development.

Mommy wants to hear about the puppies.
Susie says the make messes. They bite.
She doesn't like puppies at all.
Daddy hopes a balloon will make Susie feel better.

Balloons and breasts are too similar not to note their resemblance, especially when a little girl is giving a good bite to the nipple end. Since the baby is getting the real thing, the motive of jealousy isn't hard to imagine either. Whether Susie envies the baby who gets the breast or the mother who has them—or both—is less important than the immediate result of biting: The balloon is injured and crumpled.

Susie puts the balloon in her mouth.

She bites it very hard.

All the air comes out.

31

The currency of the unconscious is resemblances: from breasts to balloons to Mommy herself. Though dreams are disguised enough so that the dreamer is not forced to know what they are all about, they are not that clever either, especially in childhood. Susie's is transparent. She would like to bite Mommy, to deflate her, so to speak, and have Daddy to herself. The emotion of fear is part of the meaning too. This wish, Susie warns herself, is a dangerous passion.

On the next page, Susie's mother will offer her a mild, reassuring explanation of the dream. With or without such an opportunity, there are times parents must make such leaps. If we have jumped to the wrong conclusion, chances are our child will ignore our comments. So the wrong guess won't hurt. If we are right, we can help a great deal. Mommy is quite sure little girls all share such wishes; she is not angry. Perhaps it is not so dangerous after all. Just as important, Susie is put back to bed in her own room, safely away from temptation.

That night Susie has a bad dream. In the dream, Mommy had a hole in her. She crumpled up like the balloon and Daddy carried Susie away.

"Then you were alone with Daddy in the dream, weren't you? Just like you were last night," Mommy says. "Little girls like to be alone with their daddies," she explains. "Sometimes they wish their mother would crumple up and go away." Mommy does not seem angry at all. But she does not let Susie come into their bed.

In the morning,
Susie's mother
plays with her.
Susie is a puppy.
She whines
and whines and has
to be cuddled.

Then she barks and pretends to bite.
Mommy is still not angry. She does
not bite Susie back.

Susie goes with Daddy
to the bus stop again.
There is Butch. Daddy
holds on to him.
Butch will not bite Susie
either. Maybe Susie will
pat him another day.

In the days, weeks, perhaps months during which Susie is gradually recovering from her fear of dogs, much work is going on. Together, her parents work to change their behavior. Perhaps they develop a system for getting Susie to and from the bus stop in emotional safety. Maybe the bathroom is now off limits, and reading a storybook in bed substitutes for the morning cuddle session. And Susie may be encouraged to participate in the baby's care or enjoy conversation about eventual marriage and motherhood.

But the big job is still up to Susie. She must come up with a satisfactory way of including both her mother and her father in her hopes, without injury to anyone. In the atmosphere of relief and protection Susie is now experiencing, her mind is free to work at resolution.

But it takes many days before Susie can go outside alone.

Naïve as Susie's pronouncement sounds to adult ears, it is the resolution to her conflict and the final step in dropping her need of a phobia. She will defer her marriage to Daddy until she is a grown-up. Mommy need not leave, but may stay to be the grandma. And neither mother nor father will be disappointed, because a childhood wish of their own will come true: Though husband and wife, they will also be mother and son! A neat trick, and perfectly satisfying for now.

This is not really the end of this story. By next year or the year after, Daddy will be given up—though Susie's later choice of a husband may remind her of her first love in subtle ways. And some day, Daddy will reappear in his ultimate and rightful place: as Grandpa to Susie's babies.

"When I grow up and marry Daddy," Susie tells her mother, "we are going to have lots of babies. And you can be their grandma."

Maybe Mommy won't mind that so much. After all, Susie is already old enough to have a puppy.

And nobody minds that at all.